FAILED HOPE

Stories of Canada

FAILED HOPE
The Story of the Lost Peace

by John Wilson

DUNDURN
TORONTO

Editor: Cheryl Hawley
Design: Jesse Hooper
Printer: Webcom

Library and Archives Canada Cataloguing in Publication

Wilson, John (John Alexander), 1951-
    Failed hope : the story of the lost peace / by John Wilson.

Includes bibliographical references and index.
Issued also in electronic formats.
ISBN 978-1-4597-0345-2

    1. World politics--1919-1932--Juvenile literature. 2. World politics--1933-1945--Juvenile literature. 3. History, Modern--20th century--Juvenile literature. 4. Economic history--1918-1945--Juvenile literature. I. Title.

D720.W55 2012   j909.82'2   C2012-900137-6

1   2   3   4   5   16   15   14   13   12

We acknowledge the support of the **Canada Council for the Arts** and the **Ontario Arts Council** for our publishing program. We also acknowledge the financial support of the **Government of Canada** through the **Canada Book Fund** and **Livres Canada Books**, and the **Government of Ontario** through the **Ontario Book Publishing Tax Credit** and the **Ontario Media Development Corporation**.

Printed and bound in Canada.
www.dundurn.com

VISIT US AT
Dundurn.com | Definingcanada.ca | @dundurnpress | Facebook.com/dundurnpress

Dundurn
3 Church Street, Suite 500
Toronto, Ontario, Canada
M5E 1M2

Gazelle Book Services Limited
White Cross Mills
High Town, Lancaster, England
LA1 4XS

Dundurn
2250 Military Road
Tonawanda, NY
U.S.A. 14150

For the 1,600 Canadians of the Mackenzie-Papineau Battalion

THE LAST CASUALTY

For 100 days, since they had dramatically broken through the enemy lines outside Amiens on August 8, 1918, the Canadians had been pushing forward across northern France and Belgium. The Germans, their opponents at Ypres, Vimy Ridge, and Passchendaele, were almost beaten. It would soon be time to go home.

Private George Price, his mate Art Goodmurphy, and two other soldiers from A Company were carrying out a reconnaissance in the village of Ville-sur-Haine. They were chasing a German machine gun that had been harassing the troops as they crossed the nearby Canal du Centre.

It was late morning and the small squad had already flushed the machine gun from two houses when George and Art stepped out into the deserted village street. A single shot rang out and a bullet caught George square in the chest.

George Price was the last Allied soldier to die in the Great War. Ironically, he is buried in St. Symphorien Cemetery, a few graves away from Private John Parr, the first British and Commonwealth soldier to die in the war.

In the four years between Parr and Price's deaths, some 16 million people died. Almost a million were British and Commonwealth soldiers and George Price was one of 65,000 Canadians who never made it home.

The horrific casualties of the Great War convinced many people that it must never happen again. They were tragically wrong. Twenty-one years after Private Price fell on a Belgian street, all the hopes for peace had failed and the world was engaged in another war. One with casualties that would dwarf anything Price could have imagined, and with a scale that demoted the Great War to merely the First World War.

The 28th Battalion establishing a signalling HQ during the First World War.
Department of National Defence/Library and Archives Canada, PA-001096.

Art dragged his friend back into the house, where he and the Belgian family who lived there struggled to save George's life. They failed. At 10:58 that morning, a month before his 26th birthday, Private George Lawrence Price of Falmouth, Nova Scotia, died. Two minutes later, on the 11th hour of the 11th day of the 11th month, 1918, the Great War ended.

What we demand in this war ... is that the world be made fit and safe to live in; and ... that it be made safe for every peace-loving nation which ... wishes to ... be assured of justice and fair dealing by the other peoples of the world.

— President Woodrow Wilson, Speech to Congress, January 8, 1918

President Wilson's speech set out 14 points that he felt could provide a sound basis for lasting world peace. They included: arms reduction, freedom of the seas, self-determination for the many national groups in Europe, and the establishment of a League of Nations (an early version of today's United Nations) to guarantee political independence for everyone.

Council of Four at the Paris Peace Conference, May 27, 1919. Left to right: Prime Minister David Lloyd George (Great Britain), Premier Vittorio Orlando (Italy), Premier Georges Clemenceau (France), President Woodrow Wilson (United States).

U.S. Signal Corps photo.

One thing Versailles did produce was a host of new countries. Where the old Ottoman Empire had been in the Middle East, new artificial borders were created that bore little relation to the inhabitants' wishes, or their religious or cultural identities. The world is still paying the price for this today.

In Europe, Poland, Czechoslovakia, Austria, Hungary, and Yugoslavia rose from the ruins of the Austro-Hungarian Empire and from territories taken from Germany.

This was a brave attempt at President Wilson's idea of national determination, supported by the new League of Nations. Unfortunately, many of the new nations were threatened by powerful neighbours and internal disputes and, to Wilson's deep regret, his own country rejected the treaty and refused to join the League of Nations.

With extraordinary foresight, and seeing the seeds of a coming war embedded in the Treaty, French Field Marshal Ferdinand Foch declared, "This is not peace. It is an armistice for 20 years."

As commendable as Wilson's ideas were, they were not shared by the victorious European powers. The French were determined to see Germany take responsibility and pay for the war. They hoped to place so many military restrictions on Germany that it could never again threaten Europe with war.

The British were less hardline, but agreed that Germany should pay reparations for the war and were, as a major imperial power, not keen on Wilson's idea of self-determination for small nations. Even back in the United States, Wilson's own Congress wanted little to do with European affairs and only grudgingly supported the president.

The negotiations on the Treaty of Versailles got under way on January 18, 1919, in the Salle d'Horloge in Paris. The meetings of 70 delegates from 27 countries were supposed to resolve the conflicts of the Great War and provide a basis for a lasting peace. However, not everyone was in Paris. The defeated nations — Germany, Austria, and Hungary — were not invited. Neither was Russia, which had concluded a separate peace with Germany after the revolution. Instead of a rational attempt to create a peaceful world based on Wilson's 14 points, Versailles became more of a squabble among the victors as they each pursued their own agendas.

The multitude of competing demands presented at Versailles probably never could have been acceptably resolved. However, the treaty that was finally signed in the Palace of Versailles on June 28, 1919, sowed the seeds of a far greater, more horrific conflict, only a generation in the future.

GERMANY'S COST

The Treaty of Versailles declared that Germany was solely responsible for the Great War and stated that the kaiser (who had fled to the neutral Netherlands) be declared a war criminal. The German army and navy were severely limited. Submarines, tanks, armed planes, and the import or export of weapons were banned.

Germany also lost a lot of territory:

- the provinces of Alsace and Lorraine, which Germany had annexed after the Franco-Prussian War of 1870–71, were returned to France;

- the overseas Empire was divided among the Allies;

- large areas of eastern Germany were given to Poland, Czechoslovakia, and Lithuania, while other areas were annexed by Belgium and Denmark; and

- the industrial region of the Saar Basin and the city of Danzig were to be administered by the League of Nations.

Germany was also required to pay for the war. Reparations of 269 billion German gold marks (785 billion in 2011 dollars) were assessed. These were to be paid in gold, coal, steel, and intellectual property (including the trademark for aspirin).

The reparations imposed on Germany were crippling and had huge economic consequences. They also provided lingering resentment within Germany, which was skilfully used by Adolf Hitler in his rise to power.

The skull of Sultan Mkwawa.
Photo by Matt Crypto.

Not all the demands of Versaille were large-scale. Article 246 stated, "Within six months from the coming into force of the present Treaty … Germany will hand over to His Britannic Majesty's Government the skull of the Sultan Mkwawa which was removed from the Protectorate of German East Africa and taken to Germany."

Mkwawa was the chief of the Hehe tribe in German East Africa (Tanzania today). In 1891 he led a revolt against the Germans, and continued to fight them until forced to commit suicide in 1898. The British, who inherited German East Africa as part of the treaty, thought that returning the skull would be a gesture of thanks to the Hehe for supporting them during the war.

The Germans claimed that the skull could not be found and it wasn't until 1954 that Mkwawa's skull was identified in Bremen Museum and returned to Tanzania, where it is now on display.

European borders in 1918.

THE FIGHTING GOES ON

November 11th didn't mean an end to the fighting, even for Germany. Years of Allied blockade, huge casualty lists, and the obvious signs that the war was lost caused massive disaffection inside the country. The Russian Revolution of the year before seemed to show the way to change things and create a better, fairer world.

In early November 1918, sailors of the German navy stationed in Kiel mutinied and took over the town. Within days the revolt had turned into revolution across the country, as workers took control of factories, towns, and local government.

Since the abdication of the kaiser the government in Berlin had been socialist, but they were moderates. The spectre of a full-blown workers' revolution terrified them.

A rally in Berlin.
Bundesarchiv.

They called in the army to quell the revolution. Months of sporadic street fighting occurred between the revolutionaries and soldiers back from the war, who organized themselves into Free Corps (Freikorps).

Fighting in Berlin in January 1919, and the murders of the two main revolutionary leaders, Karl Liebknecht and Rosa Luxemburg, ended hope of a successful German revolution. However, fighting continued elsewhere, and it wasn't until May 3rd that the last area of revolution, the Munich Soviet Republic, was bloodily crushed.

Even while parts of Germany were immersed in what was almost civil war, parts of her army were fighting to the east.

In December 1918 Polish patriots, eager to set up their own country, rebelled against the German occupying troops. This led to weeks of fighting between the German army and the Polish nationalists, until the Treaty of Versailles confirmed the existence of the nation of Poland in 1919.

In 1919 revolutions also broke out in Egypt and Hungary, and it seemed to some that the Russian Bolshevik Revolution was about to spread Communism throughout the world. Canada was not immune to this fear.

Karl Liebknecht.

"Bolshevism Invades Canada," screamed the headlines in the *New York Times* in the spring of 1919. Cartoons of wild anarchists throwing bombs appeared in the local newspapers. Soldiers and armed police patrolled the streets of Winnipeg, scare stories about plots to overthrow the government circulated widely, and foreigners were accused of instigating violent revolution. Communist revolution seemed to have come to Canada.

At 11:00 a.m. on Thursday, May 15, 1919, 22,000 Winnipeg workers went on strike, shutting down much of the city. They weren't striking to overturn the government

Crowd gathered outside the Union Bank of Canada building on Main Street during the Winnipeg General Strike.

Library and Archives Canada, PA-163001.

The government's unwillingness to even consider the strikers' grievances, their crude attempts to deport strike leaders, and the violence used to crush the strike created much sympathy for the workers. Sympathetic strikes broke out all across Canada and the Conservative government lost the election of 1921.

In the 1921 election, the winning candidate for Winnipeg North was J.S. Woodsworth, a Methodist minister who had spoken out strongly during and after the strike. Woodsworth served his constituency until his death in 1942, and became a significant force for social change, championing medicare, old age pensions, and unemployment insurance.

In 1932, Woodsworth became the first leader of the Co-operative Commonwealth Federation (the CCF), the precursor of today's New Democratic Party.

J.S. Woodsworth addressing a meeting in 1935.
Library and Archives Canada, C-055451.

or destroy the Canadian way of life. What they wanted were wage increases to cover the postwar inflation and recognition for new unions that represented the building trade.

The government refused to negotiate with the strikers and, on June 17th, ordered the arrest of 10 strike leaders. The following Saturday, June 21st, 25,000 people gathered in Market Square to protest. Mayor Charles Gray panicked and called in the Royal Northwest Mounted Police, who charged the crowd on horseback swinging clubs and shooting. One worker died and scores were injured on what became known as "Bloody Saturday." Five days later, the biggest general strike in Canadian history was called off.

As revolutions flickered and died across the world, the Russian Bolsheviks who had inspired them were fighting for their lives. By late 1919, anti-Bolshevik armies, supported by armaments and troops from Britain, the United States, France, and several other countries, controlled vast

1918 Bolshevik propaganda poster depicting Trotsky as St. George slaying a dragon. The image of St. George and the dragon comes from the Moscow coat of arms.

Raymond Collishaw (left) and another pilot with a Sopwith Camel airplane, 1918.

Department of National Defence/Library and Archives Canada, PA-002826.

Fear of the spread of Communism led the Allies to send troops and supplies to help the White Russian cause. Part of the aid was 10 Sopwith Camel fighter planes, one of which was piloted by Canadian flying ace Raymond Collishaw. Collishaw battled the enemy and typhus, but eventually he and his colleagues abandoned their aircraft and fled on an old train.

For weeks they were chased by an armoured train that fired at them with a 9-inch cannon. They battled local Bolsheviks, who tore up the tracks in front of them, rammed them, and shot at them as they passed. In the middle of winter they had to stop to collect snow for water and wood for the engine. Another outbreak of typhus reared its head and the dead had to be thrown from the moving carriages. After the

areas of southern and eastern Russia, and were advancing on Moscow and Petrograd (known later as Leningrad and today as St. Petersburg). It looked as if the Russian Communist experiment would go the way of the German, Hungarian, and Bavarian.

However, the anti-Bolshevik, or White armies, were poorly led, poorly supplied, and torn by internal squabbles. On the other hand, the Bolsheviks, or Red Army, were politically unified, well-organized, and led by Leon Trotsky.

Trotsky, through campaigns of terror and using his remarkable organizing skills, welded the Red Army into an efficient fighting unit. As they began to fight back, the White armies retreated and disintegrated. By 1920 the war was won and, in 1923, the final outposts of anti-Bolshevism were defeated.

Not only did the Bolsheviks have to fight a civil war, they also fought a war against the new state of Poland. After the Polish uprising against the Germans, the new state annexed large areas of territory that Russia considered hers.

Polish defences near Miłosna during the Polish-Soviet War, August 1920.

While the Red Army was focussed on defeating the Whites, the Polish forces enjoyed considerable success. However, in the summer of 1920 the Red Army reached the gates of the Polish capital, Warsaw. After an eight-day battle the Poles were victorious and the Red Army forced to retreat and sue for peace. The exhausted nations agreed on a border that would remain until 1939.

survivors escaped, Collishaw admitted that his experiences in Russia were more terrifying that anything he had experienced in the Great War.

Although the Allies shared out the German overseas empire at Versailles, there were signs that all was not well, even in the largest empire of all.

In 1916, Irish nationalists had taken advantage of Britain's involvement in the war to rise in rebellion. The Easter Rebellion in Dublin had failed, but the harsh reprisals introduced by the victors, including executing the captured leaders, caused widespread anger and disgust. In sporadic violence between 1919 and 1921, hundreds of Irish fighters, police, and British soldiers died.

The Anglo-Irish Treaty, signed in December 1921, ended the war, but only offered the Irish dominion status (the same as enjoyed by Canada) and only at the cost of partitioning Ireland into the southern Irish Free State and the northern six counties that decided to stay a part of the United Kingdom.

British cavalry regiment leaving Ireland in 1922.

Disagreement between Irish who accepted dominion status and those who wanted nothing less than total freedom and a united Ireland, led to a civil war which lasted until mid-1923. The southern part of Ireland became fully independent in 1937.

On the other side of the world, Britain's empire in India was experiencing a different kind of independence movement. During the Great War, Mohandas Gandhi began

Britain was not the only country struggling with independence movements. In the early 1920s, rebellions in Spanish Morocco killed thousands before being brutally suppressed. One young officer in the Spanish army who was rapidly becoming renowned for his bravery, Francisco Franco, was promoted to the rank of general for his role in the war.

Mohandas Gandhi used non-violent civil disobedience to gain India's independence from the British Empire.

agitating for independence from Britain. Unlike the Irish, he promoted the idea of non-violence and non-cooperation with the British authorities as a way to freedom. Despite a sometimes violent reaction (as in 1919 when General Dyer ordered his soldiers to open fire on an unarmed crowd in Amritsar, killing between 400 and 1,000 men, women, and children), Gandhi and his followers stuck to his ideas of peaceful civil disobedience.

In 1930, to protest the tax on salt, Gandhi led thousands on a month-long march to the sea at Dandi, where he collected his own tax-free salt. Although the British imprisoned some 60,000 people, the protest gained worldwide attention and was a major stepping stone on the road to Indian independence in 1947.

The Great War was over but, just like today, small conflicts were breaking out in obscure corners of the world. Few people remember them now, but some had lasting consequences that we certainly know about.

Afghanistan had long been a problem for the imperial rulers of India. In 1839 an entire British army had been wiped out there, and it was the only bulwark between an expanding Russian empire and India. In 1919 Amanullah Khan came to power in Afghanistan, promising independence from the British. Using the Amritsar massacre as an excuse, he called a holy war (jihad) and crossed the Khyber Pass to invade India.

It only took a month for the British to push the Afghan army out of India, but they were loath to follow the Afghans into the treacherous mountains of their homeland. Amanullah got his independence in the subsequent peace treaty.

Nepalese soldiers in the Third Afghan War.

Another small war with far-reaching consequences occurred a year later. At Versailles, the defeated Ottoman Empire had been carved up among the victorious powers. The British were given Iraq, an artificial nation with borders drawn without any consideration for the people living there. The Iraqis rose in a revolt that was unfocussed but forced the British to establish King Faisal on the Iraqi throne.

Faisal's family ruled until overthrown by a military coup in 1958. The military ruled until the Ba'ath Party took over 10 years later. In 1979 Saddam Hussein became leader of the Ba'ath Party and president of Iraq.

Today, wars much worse than the ones in 1919 and 1920 plague Afghanistan and Iraq, but the roots of these conflicts go back to the Great War and its aftermath.

HYPERINFLATION

Imagine your mother asks you to run along to the local store and buy a loaf of bread. She gives you a five dollar bill and asks you to bring back the change. No big deal.

Imagine now that you need a truck to carry enough money along to buy that loaf of bread. That's hyperinflation and it happened in Germany in 1922 and 1923.

Germany borrowed a lot of money to pay for the Great War, and then was told to pay reparations to all the Allies who had won the war. This, combined with other aspects of the war's aftermath, such as the depletion of natural resources, and the German government simply printing more money to try and deal with the crisis, caused hyperinflation.

At the beginning of 1921 it took 60 German marks to buy one dollar. This rose to over 300 marks per dollar in 1922 and 8,000 marks per dollar by the end of the year. Prices doubled every two days and paper money became worthless.

The government printed higher and higher denomination bills, until you could get a 100 billion mark note. At that time it would cost you 4,200,000,000,000 marks to buy one dollar. It was cheaper to use paper money to wallpaper your living room than to try and buy anything with it.

Eventually things stabilized in 1923, when a new currency was issued (rentenmarks) and indexed to gold, but many people had already lost whatever savings they had and were bitter. They began looking toward a host of fringe, right-wing, nationalist parties that blamed the country's problems on the reparations payments and the German government for agreeing to pay them. Many of these parties also blamed Jewish financiers and bankers, playing on a long-standing anti-Semitism.

Germany wasn't the only country hit by hyperinflation. Austria, Hungary, Russia, and Poland all suffered about the same time. The victorious Allies didn't escape the financial cost of the war either.

Both Britain and France were financially crippled by the cost of waging total war for four years. Most of the billions of dollars of debt were to the United States, which had supplied armaments, equipment, and food throughout the war years. Much of this debt was written off, but Britain was still paying back Great War debts to America as late as 1965.

Britain and France never recovered the economic power they had enjoyed before 1914, and the United States became the dominant economic nation. Even Canada, where industry had been mobilized to supply the war, came out of the First World War relatively well off economically. The decade to come seemed to promise prosperity, if not for Europe then at least for North America.

A man using deutschmarks as wallpaper, because inflation had made them worthless.

On November 4, 1922, a bored boy scratching in the sand in the Valley of the Kings in Egypt uncovered a carved step. It led to a rubble-filled, nine-metre-long passageway that ended at a door.

Tutankhamun's burial mask, on display in the Egyptian Museum in Cairo.

Photo by Bjørn Christian Tørrissen. Licensed under the Creative Commons Attribution Share Alike 3.0 Unported license.

The moment Howard Carter opened up Tutankhamun's tomb.

Tutankhamun ruled for only nine or 10 years at a very unstable time in Egyptian history. He followed his father, Akhenaten, who had attempted to completely revolutionize Egyptian religion and society. Despite his short reign, Tutankhamun, or the advisors who looked after the child, reversed most of the changes his father had made.

On November 26, the last of the rubble was cleared from the door and an archaeologist, Howard Carter, held a candle through a small hole. As his eyes adjusted to the flickering light, Carter was struck dumb by the glint of gold from the most incredible collection of statues, furniture, and strange animals.

"Can you see anything?" Lord Carnarvon, the dig's sponsor, asked from behind.

"Yes," Carter replied, breathlessly, "wonderful things."

The tomb they had discovered was that of the boy pharaoh, Tutankhamun, who had lived his short life more than 3,000 years before. The room was filled with treasures, including the mummy of the boy king in a golden coffin.

The discovery was a sensation and exhibitions of the treasures still draw vast crowd to museums today.

Tutankhamun was a weak child, who may have walked with a limp. He was slightly built and about five feet seven inches tall when he died. He had a slight cleft palate, elongated skull, possible curvature of the spine, and severe malaria. At age 19 Tutankhamun fell and broke his leg quite badly. The break became infected. Combined with the malaria it was probably enough to kill him.

King Tut didn't live long, but, 3,000 years after he was buried, and almost a century after he was discovered, he still fascinates us.

ROARING TWENTIES

As the chaos after the Great War began to settle, economies recovered — then boomed. People began to look to the future and try to forget the horrors they had been through.

A 1920 Ford Model T.

New industries sprang up: cars became commonplace (there were 300,000 cars in Canada in 1918, almost two million in 1929); chemical industries produced a seemingly endless supply of new materials like nylon and rayon; movie palaces sprang up in every town, offering cheap entertainments

Much of the impetus for the cultural renaissance of the Roaring Twenties came from the Berlin of the Weimar Republic. Paul Klee in art; Walter Gropius and the Bauhaus school in architecture; Bertolt Brecht in theatre; Werner Heisenberg, Max Born, and Pascual Jordan in science; Fritz Lang in film; Heinrich and Thomas Mann and Erich Maria Remarque in literature, the list seems endless.

The European cultural hub of the 1920s was Paris. Many Americans, among them Ernest Hemingway, Aaron Copland, Man Ray, and Josephine Baker, moved to Paris to escape prohibition and racism at home. There they mixed with the likes of Picasso, Dali, Stravinsky, James Joyce, and a host of other avant-garde artists, musicians, and writers.

They were creating a brave new world, broken from the past and moving forward on a wave of new technology, science, and culture, toward a future where a repeat of the horrors of Passchendaele would be impossible. Unfortunately, the seeds of something even worse than Passchendaele were already being sown.

and a window to the fashions of the world; radios appeared in every home, bringing news and advertising at the turn of a dial (in early 1923 Foster Hewitt broadcast the first hockey game, the beginning of *Hockey Night in Canada*).

Twittering Machine *(Die Zwitscher Maschine) by Paul Klee, a Swiss artist who was part of the Bauhaus movement.*

As the decade progressed electricity, phone lines, indoor plumbing, and sewers reached almost everyone. For the first time in North America, more people lived in the cities than in rural areas.

The world seemed newly born out of the ashes of the Great War. Women had the vote, flappers danced the Charleston, Expressionism and Surrealism revolutionized art, jazz turned popular music on its head, dramatic Art Deco buildings were going up everywhere, Babe Ruth was hitting 60 home runs a season. Everything was less restricted, less formal, more fun than the staid world of the Victorians and Edwardians before the war. The possibilities seemed limitless.

Promo poster for Metropolis, *a science fiction film made in 1927 by Austrian director Fritz Lang.*

PROHIBITION

All across North America temperance movements, groups that believed drinking alcohol was a social evil and a sin, gained strength and support. Prince Edward Island prohibited the sale or consumption of alcohol in 1901. In 1907 Mississippi followed. But it was the Great War that gave the movement national impetus in the United States and Canada.

In 1919 Congress passed the Eighteenth Amendment to the Constitution, prohibiting the manufacture, sale, or transportation of any beverage with an alcohol content greater than 0.5 percent. This immediately destroyed the liquor, beer, and wine manufacturing industries and created a black market, mostly run by gangsters such as Al Capone.

Labour union members marching through Newark, New Jersey, in 1931, protesting prohibition.
Library of Congress, LC-USZ62-123216.

Since Canada did not enact a national prohibition law, it suddenly became very profitable to take beer and liquor south to sell. Bootleggers thrived in eastern Canada, where they could supply the tens of thousands of illegal drinking establishments (speakeasies) in Chicago and the other major cities, but smuggling went on all along the vast undefended border. On the west coast there was a running battle, among the inlets and beaches of the Gulf Islands and the Washington coast, between revenue agents and rum-runners.

As the war between gangsters to control the bootleg industry spilled onto the streets, public opinion turned against prohibition. Incidents like the murder of seven men on St. Valentine's Day 1929 shocked people and, combined with the effects of Great Depression, led to the repeal of prohibition in 1933.

Men pouring out liquor during prohibition.

Since the Eighteenth Amendment didn't specifically prohibit the consumption of alcohol, individuals found imaginative ways around the law. People drank medicinal alcohol and tried all kinds of ways to distill spirits at home. Tragically, during prohibition some 10,000 people died from the effects of drinking poisonous methyl alcohol.

Less seriously, grape-growers sold blocks of semi-solid concentrate. These were supposedly to produce grape juice. However, a warning on the label stated, "After dissolving the brick in a gallon of water, do not place the liquid in a jug away in the cupboard for twenty days, because then it would turn into wine."

Much less famous than its neighbours, Pompeii and Herculaneum, Stabiae, on the Gulf of Naples in Italy, is nevertheless rich in Roman villas buried in the 79 A.D. eruption of Mount Vesuvius. The modern town of Castellammare di Stabia has some notoriety as the hometown of Gabriele Capone, a barber and Al Capone's father.

Al was born in New York in 1899 and didn't stay out of trouble long. At 14 he was thrown out of school for violently attacking a female teacher. From this start he moved on to petty crime and small-time gangs, but it was the introduction of prohibition that gave him his opportunity for fame.

In 1924 Capone moved to Chicago to take full advantage of the corrupt city politics and the flow of illegal liquor from Canada. Soon he controlled most of the city's speakeasies, as well as gambling and prostitution. He lived a high-profile life and bribed or killed anyone who got in his way. His phrase, "I

A mug shot of Al Capone.

am just a businessman, giving the people what they want," and well-publicized donations of his illegal profits to popular charities, endeared him to many who didn't know him and earned him the reputation of being a modern-day Robin Hood.

Unable to gather enough evidence on his illegal activities, the federal government arrested and convicted Capone of tax evasion in 1931. He was sentenced to 11 years in prison, where he deteriorated both mentally and physically. He was released from Alcatraz in 1939 and died at his home in Florida in 1947. The year before his death, a psychiatrist assessed Capone as having the mental age of a 12-year-old.

On February 14, 1929, six members of Bugs Moran's rival Chicago gang, and a mechanic who was in the wrong place at the wrong time, were lined up against a garage wall and machine-gunned to death. One of the victims lived for several hours but, despite having 14 bullet wounds, insisted to police, "Nobody shot me."

Everybody knew Capone was responsible, but no one could prove it. However, the execution-style killing of so many people seriously undermined Capone's image of a Robin Hood character taking from the government and giving to the people.

HITLER'S HERO

In 1923 Adolf Hitler was in Munich, leading the small National Socialist German Workers Party (Nazi Party for short), that modelled itself on Mussolini's Fascisti. That November, Hitler tried to emulate his hero's March on Rome. The attempt ended badly, and he was arrested and imprisoned. However, it gave Hitler a national profile, and upon his release he began rebuilding the Nazi Party.

Adolf Hitler during the Nazi Party Congress of 1935.

Photograph attributed to Heinrich Hoffmann/Library and Archives Canada, PA-164749.

For disaffected people after the war, Communism was a hope for the future. But not everyone wanted to live in an egalitarian, worker-controlled state. For some of them, there was an alternative.

Mussolini (left) and Hitler, June 1940.

As a young man in Italy, Benito Mussolini was active as a revolutionary socialist, believing that change came through class war, regardless of nationality. However, in time he became disillusioned with socialism and came to believe that the nation one belonged to was what was important. In 1914 he formed a small nationalist party called Fascisti. They appealed to many people because they were both traditional and revolutionary.

In the Great War, Mussolini was wounded and promoted to corporal. After the war his small party grew rapidly, and, in 1921, Mussolini formed the National Fascist Party. In October the following year, with Mussolini at their head, the armed wing of his party, the Blackshirts, marched on Rome and staged a *coup d'état*. Mussolini became prime minister of Italy, although he had to rely on several other political parties to stay in power.

In the years following the coup, Mussolini, through a combination of threats and violence against any opposition, consolidated power until he became the absolute ruler of a one-party state. As the Roaring Twenties drew to a close, Mussolini, in complete control of Italy, dreamed of ruling an empire to rival the ancient Roman empires of Augustus and Hadrian.

Across the Alps, another ex-soldier was looking on admiringly.

Throughout the twenties, the Nazis blamed all of Germany's troubles on the Versailles Treaty and the Jews. The party gradually became better organized, and Hitler refined his ideas and his speaking techniques. However, the Nazis languished at around a dozen seats in the Reichstag, the German parliament. By 1930 they didn't appear to be going anywhere, and Hitler envied Mussolini's success in Italy. But the pupil was about to overtake the teacher.

Almost as soon as the fighting stopped in France in 1918, memorialization of the tragedy began. Tours of the battle-fields, popular with the curious and those who had lost a loved one, began almost immediately, and the Imperial War Graves Commission (IWGC) began the sad task of collecting human remains and organizing the wartime cemeteries that now dot the landscape.

In 1921, Newfoundland — at that time not yet a part of Canada — purchased 74 acres (300,000 square metres) of the ground over which the Newfoundland Regiment had attempted to advance so tragically on July 1, 1916. The trenches from which the Newfoundlanders advanced and the shell-pitted no man's land, where so many of them died, are preserved to this day. Overlooking it all is a large bronze caribou, the regiment's symbol. The Beaumont-Hamel Newfoundland Memorial was unveiled by Field Marshal Earl Haig on June 7, 1925, and is one of only two National Historic Sites of Canada located outside the country.

In 1920 the IWGC awarded Canada eight sites in France and Belgium to commemorate Canada's contribution. A commission was set up and a competition held to find a suitable memorial for the sites. The winning memorial, by sculptor and designer Walter Seymour Allward, was far too ambitious to place on every site, so it was decided to place Allward's memorial atop Vimy Ridge, and to use other designs elsewhere.

Two hundred and fifty acres (100 hectares) of land on Vimy Ridge were given to Canada by the French government "freely and for all time," for the creation of a memorial park.

Construction of the memorial began in 1925. Allward spent two years searching Europe for just the right stone for the 6,000 tonnes needed for the Vimy Memorial. He found it in the Roman emperor Diocletian's palace, in Yugoslavia (Croatia today). If the stone of Diocletian's palace could remain unweathered for 1,600 years, Allward decided it would be suitable for his memorial.

Opening of the war memorial for Newfoundland soldiers at Beaumont Hamel, France.

In January 1929, while Allward was busy at Vimy, another sort of memorialization took place in Germany. Erich Maria Remarque, who had fought as a German soldier in the war, wrote a book based on his experiences. *All Quiet on the Western Front* became an extraordinary bestseller, selling 2.5 million copies by the middle of 1930.

Remarque's stated purpose was to "tell of a generation of men who, even though they may have escaped shells, were destroyed by the war." *All Quiet on the Western Front* brought home what the war was like to millions, regardless of their nationality, and was considered an indictment against war. When Hitler and his Nazis came to power in Germany in 1933, copies of Remarque's book were burned in the streets.

One of twenty huge sculptures at the Vimy Ridge memorial — the figure of a weeping woman, mourning the fallen Canadians.

In all, the memorial took 11 years to complete. It was unveiled by King Edward VIII on July 26, 1936, in front of over 50,000 Canadian, British, and French veterans and their families.

Allward built the memorial of cast concrete, which was then covered with stone. Unfortunately, he didn't allow for movement over time and water seeped in, dissolved lime from the concrete, and deposited it on the 11,285 carved names of the Canadians who died and have no known grave. Erosion also contributed to the deterioration of the stairs and terraces of the massive memorial.

In 2005 the memorial was closed for restoration and was rededicated by Queen Elizabeth on April 9, 2007, the 90th anniversary of the battle.

Today the Vimy Memorial stands as a dramatic commemoration, to both the Canadians who died in the Great War and the increasing sense of Canadian identity and nationalism that developed in the 1920s and 30s.

The 1920s had its share of natural disasters. In 1927 the Mississippi River and its tributaries rose by as much as 17 metres over the levees, flooding 70,000 kilometres^2, causing $400,000,000 worth of damage and killing 246 people in seven states. The following year the Okeechobee hurricane raced through the Bahamas and Florida, killing over 4,000 people. Bad as these disasters were, the greatest disaster of the decade had occurred five years earlier.

Flooding at Cape Girardeau, Mississippi, in 1927.

At two minutes to noon on September 1, 1923, a magnitude 7.9 earthquake struck deep beneath Sagami Bay, south of Tokyo. The shaking from the Great Kanto Earthquake lasted for several minutes and 140,000 people died in the quake and the tsunami and fires that followed. Sixty kilometres away from the epicentre the quake was still powerful enough to move a 93-ton statue of Buddha almost two feet.

Aftermath of the 1929 Burin Tsunami, caused by the Grand Banks Earthquake.

Provincial Archives of Newfoundland and Labrador.

Canada did not escape nature's attentions. On November 18, 1929, a magnitude 7.2 quake off the south shore of Newfoundland triggered a massive underwater landslide. Three hours later, a series of three- to four-metre tsunami came ashore at speeds of up to 105 kilometres per hour.

The Grand Banks Earthquake produced the only recorded tsunami to have struck Canada's east coast. Twenty eight people died and 10,000 more were made homeless. Relief efforts were seriously hampered by a blizzard that struck the following day.

Because the earthquake happened at lunchtime, many people were cooking over open fires. In the aftermath, the fires spread out of control, destroying huge areas of Tokyo and Yokohama. In Tokyo, 38,000 people sought refuge in a large space that had been an army clothing depot. As the firestorm grew, a huge fire tornado formed, killing all 38,000 within fifteen minutes.

Earthquake destruction from Kanto earthquake in Yokohama.

Harsh as nature could be, people still managed to make things worse. After the quake, wild stories about foreigners, particularly Koreans, looting, robbing, and poisoning wells spread. Several thousand Koreans and other ethnic minorities were murdered by angry mobs.

SCOPES TRIAL

On March 21, 1925, the Butler Act came into law in Tennessee. It prohibited school teachers from denying the Biblical story of human origins and forbade the teaching of evolution in schools.

Almost immediately, the American Civil Liberties Union began looking for ways to challenge the law. John T. Scopes, a football coach who sometimes did substitute teaching, agreed to act as defendant.

John Scopes.

An eight-day trial, featuring two of the biggest legal names in the country, ex-presidential candidate William Jennings Bryan and famous defence attorney Clarence Darrow, received national publicity. The trial pitted fundamentalists, who thought that the words of the bible should have precedence over science, against those who saw no conflict between religion and evolution.

Scopes was found guilty and fined $100, but his conviction was overturned on appeal on a technicality. The Butler Act remained on the law books of Tennessee until 1967.

After the trial, Scopes admitted that he had never actually taught evolution in class and that the lawyers had coached his students. It also came out that much of the support for the trial was from local businessmen who thought the publicity it generated would be good for their town of Dayton.

Despite Scopes being found guilty, the trial became a byword for the battle between evolution and creationism, a battle that continues in many places today. In 2006 a high school science teacher in northern Quebec was repeatedly told by his school principal not to teach evolution because it hurt his grade 7 and 8 students' religious beliefs. A 2009 poll showed that only 58 percent of Canadians accepted evolution.

The Great War pushed technological advances ahead at a breakneck pace. After the war the pace slowed, but the 1920s were still a time of dramatic change.

One of the most famous inventions of the time was actually developed too late to be used in the war. The Thompson submachine gun, or Tommy gun, was first offered for sale in 1919 and rapidly became popular with police forces and prohibition gangsters alike.

Zeppelins, lighter-than-air flying machines, were invented in Germany before the war, but used extensively for bombing raids on Britain and France. After the war, Versailles banned Zeppelins in Germany. But the ruling was eventually relaxed and in 1929 the Graf Zeppelin circumnavigated the world in just over 21 days.

The LZ 127 Graf Zeppelin.

Photo by Alexander Cohrs, 1930. Licensed under the Creative Commons Attribution Share Alike 3.0 Unported Licence.

Although people had been working on transmitting pictures electronically, Scottish inventor John Logie Baird demonstrated the first television in 1926. The following year, he developed the first video recording system. The 1920s also saw the first Technicolor movies.

Aircraft had developed radically during the war and this continued with the introduction of mail delivery flights and passenger transport. The first non-stop crossing of the Atlantic was completed as early as 1919 by John Alcock and Arthur Whitten Brown in a Vickers Vimy bomber. Other firsts followed in quick succession, including Charles Lindbergh's first solo crossing in 1927.

Many of the new inventions of the interwar years, like the Tommy gun, had violent uses. However, the greatest discovery of the time could be used only for good, and it was Canadian. In 1922 Frederick Banting and Charles Best discovered insulin, enabling the first effective treatment for diabetes. The following year, Banting and J.J.R. Macleod, in whose lab at the University of Toronto Banting worked, were awarded the Nobel Prize for Medicine. Banting thought this unfair and gave half his prize money to his assistant, Best.

Frederick Banting (right) and Charles Best (left), the discoverers of insulin.
Library and Archives Canada, C-001350.

Charles Best nearly had nothing to do with Banting's work. In the summer of 1922, Banting only needed one lab assistant and there were two students available, Best and Clark Noble. To decide who would work with Banting, the pair tossed a coin. Best won the toss and fame as the co-discoverer of insulin.

Canada ended the 1920s in good shape. Wheat prices were high and production was increasing, so prairie farmers were doing well and investing their profits in new machinery and trucks. Canadian pulp exports equalled those of the rest of the world combined, bringing in foreign exchange and providing jobs. In 1929 few people worried about the forests being cut down.

Canada was close to becoming the second largest producer of hydro power in the world. Hydroelectricity powered factories and homes across the country and into the United States. Oil and gas discoveries in Alberta and new mining ventures on the Canadian Shield were creating new jobs and wealth.

Logging on Vancouver Island, circa 1930.
Library and Archives Canada, PA-040944.

Wingham Hydro-Electric Plant, Wingham, Ontario (circa 1923).
Library and Archives Canada, PA-031403.

The Group of Seven painters were producing distinctly Canadian art, the Royal Canadian Air Force was formed, Mount Logan, the highest mountain in Canada, was climbed for the first time, and old age pensions were introduced.

Of course, it was not all rosy, as the Winnipeg strike had proved. The Victoria school board tried to implement separate schools for the Chinese; Chinese immigration, apart from businessmen, diplomats, and students, was banned; and 56 percent of students in Saskatchewan were found to be infected with tuberculosis. Overall, though, life was good and would only get better.

In 1928 the IX Olympics were held in Amsterdam. Canada won four gold medals that summer. Ethel Catherwood won the women's high jump and Smith, Rosenfeld, Cook, and Bell won the women's 4x100 metres relay.

The huge surprise of the games, for Canadians and everyone else, was a 20-year-old lad from Vancouver, Percy Williams. Williams beat the odds to win gold in both the men's 100-metre and 200-metre races. He returned home a hero. Williams continued running, setting a world record for the 100-metre in 1930. Sadly, an injury cut his career short and he lived for many years with painful arthritis. In 1982, Percy Williams shot himself with a gun he had been awarded for his 1928 Olympic achievements.

Percy Williams of Canada (right) competing in the 1924 Summer Olympic Games in Paris, France.
Library and Archives Canada, PA-151015.

As the 1920s became the 1930s, people could look back with a certain amount of pride and forward with considerable hope. The postwar economic depression had turned into mostly booming economies, and inflation was under control. The League of Nations, despite no American involvement, had intervened successfully in a number of minor border disputes. The revolutionary movements inspired by the Russian Revolution seemed to have petered out. Disarmament was an increasingly popular topic and several international agreements — the Kellog-Briand Pact of 1928, for example — renounced war as a way of settling national disputes.

Unfortunately, there were dark clouds on the horizon.

In 1911 a revolution in China had overthrown 2,000 years of imperial rule and established a republic. In 1927 the Communist Party, including a young firebrand called Mao Zedong, split from the government, beginning a civil war. At first, few outside China took any notice of the squabbles in the remote corners of that vast and mysterious country. Soon they would have to.

After Vladimir Lenin, the leader of the Russian Revolution of 1917, died in 1924, a power struggle resulted in the rise to power of Joseph Stalin. Stalin

Mao Zedong, leader of the Chinese Revolution.

Portrait attributed to Zhang Zhenshi (1914–92) and a committee of artists.

began centralizing Russian agriculture and industry, and seemed to be rationalizing the chaos of the long civil war. Unknown to most, Stalin's opponents were beginning to disappear mysteriously.

A group of participants in the 8th Congress of the Russian Communist Party, 1919. In the middle are Stalin, Vladimir Lenin, and Mikhail Kalinin.

Throughout October 1929 stock prices collapsed. They continued falling for several weeks, but that November prices appeared to bottom out. A gradual recovery dominated the first months of 1930. The worst was over, wasn't it?

In the elections of September 1930, Adolf Hitler's Nazi Party jumped from 12 to 107 seats in the Reichstag. Suddenly the racist rabble-rouser was more than just a vaguely amusing fringe figure.

If the 1920s were an upward journey of hope, the 1930s were a downward spiral toward another horrific war. Beginning with the collapse of the economy.

Hitler (left) standing behind future Luftwaffe leader Hermann Göring, at a Nazi rally in Nuremberg (circa 1928).

GREAT DEPRESSION

*Stock prices have reached what looks like
a permanently high plateau.*

— IRVING FISHER, ECONOMIST, SHORTLY BEFORE THE STOCK MARKET CRASH OF 1929

If you were making money in the booming economy of the Roaring Twenties, and wanted to see your savings grow through investment, chances are you would have put your money in the stock market. Stocks were continually increasing in value and it seemed that every week your savings were increasing. Then came Black Thursday.

On October 24, 1929, the value of shares on the New York Stock Exchange collapsed. All those saving that had been growing for months vanished overnight.

The trading floor of the New York Stock Exchange just after the crash of 1929.

In Canada the gross national product dropped by 40 percent in the decade after 1929 — exports vanished, profits dropped, businesses closed. By 1933 almost 30 percent of the workforce was unemployed, and one fifth of the population depended on government assistance.

Primary industries, like farming, mining, and logging, suffered dreadfully as prices for commodities fell and trade restrictions abroad cut into markets.

The effects of the Depression weren't uniform across the country. Western Ontario, with its automotive and steel plants, was hard hit, as were the Prairies with their reliance on collapsing wheat prices. On top of everything else, an unusually wet period on the plains ended in 1930. Most people thought that dry year was just an exception. They were soon proved horribly wrong.

The slide had begun in September and would continue into mid-November. Then there was a recovery into 1930 that brought share prices back to the levels of early 1929, but it was a false hope.

The slide continued, people lost all their savings and, more importantly for the economy, lost confidence in the financial system. People stopped spending and hoarded money. Industry slowed down, production dropped, banks failed, and unemployment rose. Governments tried to stem the panic by introducing trade restrictions to protect their own industries and agriculture, but mostly what that did was to spread the depression around the world. Then the dust bowl hit the Midwest.

Newspaper from the day after the crash of 1929.

DUST BOWL

At first the huge, roiling black cloud on the western horizon sparked hope. Perhaps this was the long-awaited rain that would end the drought. But something was wrong. The cloud was low and moving very fast. All at once the world disappeared in a swirling mass of thick dust. Visibility dropped to a metre or two, and the wind and dust got in through every crack in barn and house walls, stinging eyes and choking throats. Then it passed, leaving the dried-out wheat fields looking more like a desert than a farm.

The dust in these storms that raced across vast areas of the Canadian and American Midwest in the 1930s was topsoil, blowing off wheat fields that had been over-farmed and had not seen rain for too long. The dust blew from west to east, landing like snow as far away as Chicago, New York, and Washington. Sometimes the storms were followed by thick clouds of locusts that ravaged anything that was left. To prairie farmers, it seemed almost like they were suffering the wrath of a vengeful god.

The Single Men's Unemployed Association parading to Bathurst Street United Church, Toronto (circa 1930).
Library and Archives Canada, C-029397.

In Canada, the Conservative government of R.B Bennett at first refused to provide aid to the provinces hardest hit by the Depression and Dust Bowl. Eventually, they introduced relief building programs and work camps, but they were not well run and provided a fertile breeding ground for activists spreading communist ideas (see "On to Ottawa").

Bennett's poor attempts to copy Roosevelt's New Deal failed. In 1935, using the slogan

A dust storm hits Stratford, Texas, in 1935.

"King or Chaos," William Lyon Mackenzie King's Liberals swept back into power. By then the effects of the Great Depression were easing but, as in the United States, it took the rearmament of the Second World War for the economy of Canada to return to 1929 levels.

Unprofitable farms were repossessed by banks or simply abandoned by desperate families. In the United States, in addition to the 500,000 people left homeless by the storms, the 1930s saw some 2.5 million people move off the land into cities or out to California.

In 1933, Franklin D. Roosevelt became president and instituted a series of relief programs, termed the New Deal. Measures were taken to educate farmers about soil conservation and relief was provided for the most distressed areas. A belt of 200 million trees were planted from the Canadian border to Texas to help break the wind and hold soil in place.

In the United States, work was provided for projects like the tree planting through the Civilian Conservation Corps (CCC). Work camps were set up and young men and their families were paid for a wide variety of work across the country. In all, about 2.5 million passed through the program.

Projects like the CCC and farmer education helped, but it wasn't until the rains returned and the economy bounced back during the Second World War that things improved for many people.

Prohibition gave gangsters like Al Capone their chance, but the Depression and Dust Bowl spawned a different kind of criminal. Heavily armed robbers like John Dillinger, Pretty Boy Floyd, and Baby Face Nelson criss-crossed the country stealing cars, holding up banks, and robbing stores. Many of them became household names, but the two with the most lasting fame were Bonnie and Clyde.

Clyde Barrow was a small-time thief in Texas, until he spent two years in Eastham Prison Farm from 1930 to 1932. There he was brutally abused and came out a bitter killer, vowing revenge on the police and the prison system.

Bonnie Parker was a smart student who did well in school, but she dropped out to get married at age fifteen. After her marriage broke up, she met Clyde at a friend's house in 1930. She fell in love and waited for him to get out of prison. In the summer of 1932 they embarked on their short, famous life of crime.

Joined by Clyde's brother, Buck, and Buck's wife, Blanche, they roamed through Texas, Indiana, Louisiana, and Minnesota, robbing banks and killing anyone who got in their way. They were cornered twice but managed to shoot their way out. The second time, in July 1933, Buck was mortally wounded and Blanche arrested.

Bonnie and Clyde kept running, even staging a daring breakout from Eastham. As the killings mounted (Clyde probably killed at least nine officers and several civilians), the net around them tightened. They died in a hail of bullets on a rural road in Louisiana on May 23, 1934.

Snapshot of criminal Bonnie Parker that was seized by police. This photo contributed greatly to the Bonnie and Clyde mythology.

What captured the public's imagination were a collection of photographs that were found after Bonnie and Clyde had fled one of their hideouts. They showed the couple clowning around and posing with their substantial armoury of weapons. One photo that hit the front pages of newspapers across the country showed an attractive Bonnie Parker posing provocatively by a car with a revolver on her hip and a cigar clenched between her teeth. With the photographs were several poems that Bonnie had written.

Bonnie didn't smoke cigars and there is no evidence that she ever shot anyone, but the image of the good-looking, hardened gangster's moll with the poetic side stuck. The killers came to represent the devil-may-care freedom that so many longed for in the dark days of the Depression.

Bonnie Parker and Clyde Barrow, sometime between 1932 and 1934.
United States Library of Congress's Prints and Photographs division, digital ID cph.3c34474.

Early in 1930, Hitler's brownshirts rampaged through Berlin, smashing shop windows and beating up anyone who looked Jewish. Eight Jews died, the first of the millions who would die in the coming decade and a half.

Hitler, at the window of the Reich Chancellery, receives an ovation on the evening of his inauguration as chancellor, January 30, 1933.
Bundesarchiv.

Even though the Nazis were the second largest party in the Reichstag after the elections of 1930, they refused to form a coalition government unless Hitler was made chancellor. Instead they kept up their violence, intimidating those who opposed them and fighting running battles in the streets with Communists.

Germany wasn't the only country where people were dying in the streets. Across the Atlantic there was a new killer on the loose. In 1931, 30,000 Americans, only a few less than the number who died in France in the Great War and far more than the Nazis were killing in Germany, died in automobile accidents. The car, and all the things that came with it, was here to stay.

The aftermath of a car accident.
Library of Congress Prints and
Photographs Division Washington, D.C.
20540 USA.

Nazi leaders spoke violently against the Versailles Treaty in favour of a greater Germany, and blamed the world's woes on Jews. Their rabble-rousing appealed to the millions of unemployed who felt helpless and were looking for someone to blame.

In the 1932 elections the Nazis became the largest national party in Germany, but still refused a role in government unless they were given complete power. Nazi power also increased in local elections, but all this merely led to more violence as brownshirts rampaged everywhere, fighting in the streets and murdering hundreds of opponents across the country.

In the 1932 elections for German president, Field Marshal Hindenburg won with 19 million votes. The Communist candidate, Ernst Thaelmann, came a distant third, but everyone looked at Hitler, who came second with a staggering 13 million votes.

Paul von Hindenburg, president of Germany from 1925 until his death in 1934, and Adolf Hitler.
Bundesarchiv.

Germany was sliding into chaos, and behind the scenes the government was quietly building up the army with the help of Sweden and Russia. Winston Churchill's son, Randolph, after a visit to Germany, observed that Germany was "determined once more to have an army. I am sure that once they have achieved it they will not hesitate to use it."

TURNING POINT — 1933

... the only thing we have to fear is fear itself.
— FRANKLIN ROOSEVELT, INAUGURAL ADDRESS

Roosevelt became president promising hope and a way out of the economic chaos of the Depression. Elsewhere things were not so optimistic.

In China the Nationalist government was fighting a brutal war against Mao's Communists. While the League of Nations looked on helplessly, Japan had invaded Manchuria the year before and set up a puppet emperor.

In Spain strikes swept the country, anarchists threw bombs, and riots in Barcelona killed several people. The Spanish Republic had only existed for two years, but already it was in trouble. Elections at the end of the year swept right-wing parties into power.

A dreadful, state-caused famine was sweeping Russia as dissidents were put on public trial before disappearing into the horrors of the Siberian camps. An estimated 200,000 slave labourers died on the construction of the White Sea-Baltic Canal and Stalin's secret police were more powerful and feared than ever. But in 1933 all eyes were on Germany.

On January 30th, President Hindenburg offered Adolf Hitler, as the leader of the largest party in the Reichstag, the office he had been demanding for years, chancellor of Germany. Effectively, this gave the Nazis control of the government and they wasted no time in using it.

In February, Jews were expelled from Berlin University and the offices of the Communist Party, and all pacifist organizations were closed. A fire in the Reichstag was used to bring in rules legalizing imprisonment without trial, followed by mass arrests and torture of opponents. Those arrested were sent to new camps, the first of which was Dachau outside Munich.

Anyone who spoke out against the Nazis was intimidated, non-Nazi newspapers were banned, and the offices of opposition political parties were raided, their files destroyed and the names of members stolen. The tentacles of the Nazi

Firemen work on the burning Reichstag, February 1933.
Bundesarchiv.

The Nazi anthem, heard everywhere after 1933, was called the Horst Wessel Song.

Horst Wessel was a young Nazi who was killed in 1930 and held up as a martyr. In fact, he was shot in a Berlin apartment by a Communist as part of what was probably a squabble over prostitutes. The landlady tried to get a doctor to tend to the seriously wounded Wessel, but another Nazi refused to let the doctor in because he was Jewish. Wessel's friend said it would be better for the 22-year-old Nazi to die than be treated by a Jew. Six weeks later Wessel did die from his wound, and was turned into a hero.

Horst Wessel.
Bundesarchiv.

dictatorship spread into every corner of German life, while Hitler, Goebbels, and Göring ranted on about the dangers of Communists and Jews. In March, Hitler forced the Enabling Act through the Reichstag. This gave the Nazis almost total power. Democracy in Germany came to an end.

The airship R101.

Throughout the 1920s many countries followed Germany's lead in developing lighter-than-air vehicles. Britain was particularly interested, as Zeppelins had a much longer range than regular aircraft and could be used to carry passengers, soldiers, and supplies around her far-flung empire. Two new aircraft, the R100 and R101, were designed.

The R101 was the largest airship of its time and was innovative in many ways, perhaps too many ways. She proved difficult to handle on test flights and leaked the hydrogen that filled her gas bags. Nevertheless, her maiden voyage to India was approved.

The R101 left Cardington, England, on the evening of October 4, 1930, with 55 passengers and crew on board. Almost immediately things went wrong, and observers on the ground were worried to see her flying too low over England and northern France.

The following day, in a rainstorm near Beauvais, France, the R101 went into a slow dive and crashed. She caught fire and burned for almost 24 hours. Forty-eight people on board died, more than in the much more famous *Hindenburg* disaster in 1937.

The R100 was less innovative but much safer and more successful. In July 1930 she crossed the Atlantic in 78 hours, at an average speed of 68 kilometres per hour. Over 100,000 people visited her in the 12 days she was moored at St. Hubert, Quebec, and a number took a 24-hour flight over Ottawa, Toronto, and Niagara Falls. In August the R100 returned successfully to Britain.

The R101 disaster spelled the end of airships in Britain, and the R100 was sold for scrap in 1931.

The wreckage of R101 airship.

If, during the Depression in Canada, you were single, unemployed, and male you had two choices. You could scrounge, beg, or steal enough to live on, or you could go to Prime Minister Bennett's military-run relief camps.

In the camps, at least in theory, you received three meals a day, medical care, and 20 cents per day for your labour. It was better than starving, but the conditions were harsh, food was often bad, and there was no prospect of anything better. Many of the men in the camps thought of them as little better than prisons to get the unemployed off the city streets.

In an attempt to improve conditions, especially after the men saw the beginnings of Roosevelt's New Deal in the United States, the Relief Camp Worker's Union was set up. As conditions worsened in the camps, the union decided on a strike to

Men in a relief camp, 1933.

Department of National Defence/ Library and Archives Canada, PA-035128.

If you were unemployed and wanted to get somewhere in the 1930s, you usually walked. Hitchhiking worked in rural areas for short trips, but people didn't travel as much or as far by car as they do today. The best way to travel any great distance for free was "on the freights."

Freight trains travelled slowly, especially on hills and corners, and sat for long periods in sidings. It was relatively easy to slip into an empty wagon or boxcar. Then you waited and endured a very uncomfortable journey to your destination. Particularly unpleasant aspects of travelling this way were the thick, choking smoke in the kilometres long tunnels in the Rockies and the bitter cold in all except the height of summer. It wasn't fun but, if you were lucky, there might be work at the end of it.

call attention to the men's plight. In April 1935, calling for work and wages, most of the 2,000 men in British Columbia's work camps went on strike.

The men left the camps and headed for Vancouver to make their case visible. They demonstrated, marched through the streets, collected money from sympathetic passersby, and briefly took over the Vancouver Museum. They held rallies in major department stores to plead their case to shoppers. However, when they did this in the Hudson's Bay Company store, the manager called the police. Vancouver police and Mounties, wielding clubs, tried to force the men out of the store, and a battle broke out in the streets.

The fight at the Bay was the only violence during the strike, but it soon became obvious that Bennett's government was going to continue ignoring the strikers' requests for a hearing. Then, at a union meeting in June, someone suggested taking the message directly to the politicians in Ottawa. It was a radical idea, but the image of thousands of ragged, unemployed men on the cultivated lawns of Parliament Hill was powerful. The On to Ottawa Trek was born.

Relief Project No. 40. Wagonload of labourers.
Department of National Defence/Library and Archives Canada, PA-142914.

ON TO OTTAWA

On June 3 and 4, 1935, some 1,500 men climbed onto the roofs of freight cars or into open freight wagons in Vancouver and headed east. Thousands of Vancouverites came out to cheer them on their way. As word spread ahead of what was being called the On to Ottawa Trek, more men joined. In Golden, British Columbia, a local woman with a bathtub full of stew over a roaring fire fed the trekkers. Despite the cold, discomfort, and tunnels, spirits rose. How could the government ignore something this big? Then the trains pulled into Regina.

Strikers en route to eastern Canada during the On to Ottawa Trek, 1935.
Library and Archives Canada, C-029399.

Prime Minister Bennett, nervous about thousands of ragged trekkers showing up in Ottawa, ordered the freights stopped in Regina. Without the trains, the trekkers were stuck. They camped out on the Regina Exhibition grounds and waited, while eight of their leaders went to meet Bennett on Parliament Hill.

The meeting did not go well. The men put forward their grievances and Bennett accused them of being agitators and railed against the "Communist menace." As the trekkers left with nothing accomplished, one of them noticed the black boots of a Mountie sticking out from behind a curtain. Bennett didn't want to take any chances with these rough-looking men.

When they returned to Regina, the men found that 350 Mounties were patrolling the city. The leaders called a meeting in Market Square on the evening of July 1 to tell the trekkers what had happened in Ottawa. Hundreds of trekkers attended, as well as large numbers of curious Regina citizens, including women and children. In the middle of the speeches, at a whistled signal, baseball bat–wielding Regina police and RCMP officers arrested the speakers, formed a line, and advanced on the crowd.

Prime Minister R.B. Bennett.
Library and Archives Canada, C-000687.

The trekkers and local citizens defended themselves as best they could. For several hours a running battle filled the Regina streets. When the gas and dust cleared, some 250 people had been injured, several with police bullet wounds, and one man, a plainclothes policeman shot by mistake, was dead. Stories abounded about trekkers being shot and their bodies dragged away, but they were never confirmed. What was certain was that the Regina Riot signalled the end of the On to Ottawa Trek.

In October 1935, Bennett was swept from power in a general election. The new prime minister, William Lyon Mackenzie King, improved conditions in the work camps. This helped, but the Depression didn't go away and, in any case, events in Europe were beginning to gather momentum toward events that would swamp the concerns of a few thousand workers in Canada.

FASCISM VS. COMMUNISM

One of the reasons that the Nazis managed to come to power in Germany was the struggle between the competing ideologies of Fascism and Communism. Both Fascism on the political right and Communism on the political left had grown out of the Great War and the chaos of the 1920s, and both were totalitarian and hated democracy. The upheavals of two decades — war, revolution, and economic collapse — convinced many people that democracy wasn't working.

The extreme parties seemed to offer a simple answer. The Communists offered a state where all were equal and the workers would control the products of their labour. The Fascists offered national pride, a centralized economy, stability, and security. Although it wasn't always obvious, the promises of both turned out to be lies, but by the early 1930s

A 1937 Nazi anti-Bolshevism poster.

Soviet propaganda poster depicting Hitler as a dirty rat.

there were few people left in Germany and elsewhere who were prepared to fight to preserve democracy.

Even in the early 1930s, many people saw a war coming between Fascism and Communism. It was time to take sides, but which side would the democracies of Britain, France, the United States, and Canada take?

Both culturally and historically, Japan had developed along a different path from Europe. However, throughout the decades after the Great War, the Japanese became more and more militaristic. It wasn't fascism, but it shared many of the same characteristics: extreme nationalism, a centralized economy, and a totalitarian government.

Prime Minister William Lyon Mackenzie King.

Library and Archives Canada, C-000387.

Many politicians, like Prime Minister Mackenzie King, were prepared to let Hitler get away with so much because they feared communism more. As late as June 1937, long after the Nazis had introduced severe laws against Jews, crushed any opposition, and made it obvious that they had designs on large areas of surrounding countries, King visited Germany. He was not bothered by the obvious anti-Semitism and called the visit, "… enjoyable, informative, and inspiring."

One of the major factors in Hitler's consolidation of power in 1933 was the failure of those who should have opposed him to take a stand.

The Nazis carried out a brutal campaign of terror against their obvious enemies, the Communists and trade unions, but other segments of German society that should have stood up to them didn't. The German civil service, the army, the law profession, and the Catholic and Protestant churches either supported the Nazis or folded when faced with any intimidation. Had any or all of these groups stood up to the Nazi grab for power, Hitler would have had a much harder time establishing his totalitarian state.

Unfortunately, those outside Germany were little better. Isolated voices, like Winston Churchill, spoke out against what was happening in Germany, but most of the democracies clung to the belief that Hitler was reasonable and

British Prime Minister Winston Churchill.

Yousuf Karsh/Library and Archives Canada, PA-165806.

would settle down if given what he wanted. It was a fatal mistake and was to have dire consequences as the decade wore on.

Of his meeting with Hitler, King wrote, "He smiled very pleasantly and indeed had a sort of appealing and affectionate look in his eyes ... he is really one who truly loves his fellow man." He went on to compare Hitler to Joan of Arc. King could hardly have been more wrong.

SINO-JAPANESE WAR

As Canada and the rest of the world sat back and watched Germany, war was already breaking out in the Far East.

Japan saw neighbouring China as a rich source of raw materials, and since the end of the 19th century had been increasing its influence there. There was considerable fighting after Japan invaded Manchuria in 1931, but full-scale war did not erupt until 1937, when the Japanese captured Beijing, Shanghai, and Nanking.

A Japanese soldier executes a Chinese civilian during the Nanking Massacre.

After Nanking was captured, a campaign of systematic brutality resulted in the deaths of as many as 300,000 civilians. The Nanking Massacre shocked the world, but it was not an isolated incident in this horrific war. In all, some 20 million Chinese became casualties between 1937 and the war's end in 1945.

Mao Zedong and Chiang Kai-shek with United States Ambassador Patrick J. Hurley, 1945.

In China, the Japanese faced a disorganized and poorly supplied enemy. The Chinese government, the Kuomintang (KMT) under Chiang Kai-shek, controlled only a small area of the country. The rest was ruled by a collection of local warlords, each pursuing their own personal goals. This allowed the Japanese to defeat them piecemeal, and even to make treaties with some.

The one group that fought relentlessly against the Japanese invaders, even while fighting off attacks by the KMT, was the Chinese Communist Party. Under Mao Zedong, they fought a guerrilla war that gave them the experience to win against the KMT in the late 1940s, after the Japanese were defeated.

AMELIA

On May 21, 1932, a bright red Lockheed Vega 5b aircraft bumped to a stop in field at Culmore, Northern Ireland. A young woman in a flying suit climbed down. A local farmhand approached and inquired, "Have you flown far?" The woman flashed a gap-toothed smile and replied, "From America." Amelia Earhart had just become the first woman to fly solo across the Atlantic Ocean.

Amelia Earhart was a household name in the late 1920s and early 30s. She broke countless flying records, went on lecture tours, spoke out for the Equal Rights Amendment, wrote bestselling books, and promoted distinctive lines of clothing and luggage.

Amelia Earhart with a Lockheed Model 10E Electra, circa 1937.

In 1937 Earhart and navigator Fred Noonan set off on an attempt to circumnavigate the world in a twin-engine Lockheed Model 10E Electra. On July 2 they took off from Lae, New Guinea, heading for Howland Island, a tiny sliver of land over 4,000 kilometres away.

Later that morning the United States Coast Guard cutter *Itasca*, stationed near Howland, picked up strong radio transmissions from the Electra. However, the transmissions faded and Earhart and Noonan were never seen again.

What happened to Amelia Earhart remains a mystery. Probably, they ran out of fuel shortly after missing Howland Island and crashed in the ocean. Intriguingly, possibly human bones, enigmatic radio signals, a campsite, and fragments of metal that might have come from a Lockheed Electra have been found on Gardner Island (now Nikumaroro), suggesting that Earhart flew some 350 miles south of Howland and crashed there before she and Noonan succumbed to starvation. Whatever happened, Amelia Earhart fascinates people to this day.

OLYMPICS

In 1931, when Germany was still a republic, the 1936 Summer Olympic Games were awarded to Berlin. By 1936 Hitler had consolidated power in Germany by eliminating opposition, both outside and inside the Nazi Party. The Olympics were the perfect opportunity to show the world how wonderful the new Germany was.

Forty-nine nations participated in Berlin (Spain and the Soviet Union boycotted the games), and Germany dominated the medals, winning 33 gold, 26 silver, and 30 bronze. Basketball was introduced and, in the final, the United States defeated Canada 19–8 on an outside dirt court in driving rain. But it is politics and racism that the event is remembered for.

Jesse Owens on the podium after winning the long jump at the 1936 Summer Olympics. On podium (left to right): Naoto Tajima, Owens, Luz Long.
Bundesarchiv.

Prior to the games, the Nazis removed the signs that forbade Jews from going into the major Berlin tourist attractions. They arrested and imprisoned hundreds of Romany people, and did not allow German Jewish athletes to participate. The United States even removed the two Jewish sprinters from their relay team so as not to embarrass Hitler.

Jesse Owens at the start of his record-breaking 200-metre race at the Berlin Olympics, 1936.

Library of Congress, Reproduction Number: LC-USZ62-27663.

Berlin beat out Barcelona to host the games. In protest at the Olympics being held in Nazi Germany, Spain hosted a People's Olympiad in Barcelona from July 19 to 26, 1936.

Six thousand athletes from 22 nations, including exiles from Germany and Italy, and Canadians who boycotted Berlin, registered to compete. The usual sports were scheduled as well as chess, dancing, music, and theatre events.

Unfortunately, the Barcelona Olympiad never happened. The day before they were due to begin, the Spanish army staged a coup against the government. The games were cancelled and the athletes went home, with the exception of some 200 who stayed to fight in a war that many saw as a desperate attempt to stop the spread of Fascism.

Jesse Owens, a black American sprinter and long jumper, won four gold medals and the world press trumpeted the fact that Hitler had refused to shake his hand. In fact, Hitler shook no one's hand after the first day of competition, because he had to show neutrality. Jesse Owens claimed that Hitler had waved to him and was upset that President Roosevelt never sent him a telegram of congratulations. Ironically, in Berlin, Owens was free to use public transit and enter bars and restaurants without any of the trouble that would have caused in much of the United States.

THE SPANISH REPUBLIC

In 1931 the Spanish king, Alfonso XIII, bowed to popular pressure, abdicated, and went into exile. The troubled eight-year history of the Spanish Republic began.

Elections in 1931 brought in a left-wing government determined to limit the vast power of the Catholic Church in Spain, redistribute land from rich landowners to landless peasants, give women the vote, legalize divorce, cut the size of the army, and generally create a fairer society. The reforms they introduced, which we would take for granted today in Canada, were met with violent opposition from the political right and led to a failed army revolt in 1932.

Hitler meets General Francisco Franco at Hendaye, France, in 1940.

In the mid-1930s, all across the world, people were turning away from the ballot box and toward the political extremes, left and right, in search of a solution to the problems they faced.

The left was triumphant in Russia and the right in Germany, Italy, and Japan. France and Spain teetered between the two extremes. Only in Britain, Canada, and the United States did democracy hang on, but even there they were under pressure from growing Communist and Fascist parties.

The democracies seemed powerless and many thousands of people, both refugees from the extremist nations and concerned people elsewhere, saw the world collapsing into totalitarianism and felt powerless to do anything. What was about to happen in Spain gave them an opportunity to do something. However, it was an opportunity that would cost many their lives.

Elections at the end of 1933 brought in a right-wing government that, using army units under General Francisco Franco, brutally suppressed workers' uprisings in northern Spain and tried to undo all the advances that the previous government had made. In February 1936 the left-wing parties unified in the Popular Front and won the subsequent elections.

Both the left and right feared each other and Spain became plagued by riots, strikes, and political murder. On July 17 and 18, 1936, the army staged a coup. The coup was defeated in most major cities across Spain, but it succeeded in Spanish Morocco, where it was led by General Franco.

A Spanish Republican propaganda poster warning of the dangers of Franco's Fascist allegiances.

Franco's rebellion quickly captured the south and west of Spain. In early November 1936 he launched an attack on Madrid. In brutal fighting and beneath the slogan "They Shall Not Pass," the hastily assembled Republican army held off the Nationalist attacks, sometimes fighting an enemy in the next room of a building. They were helped by some 3,000 foreign volunteers, mostly German and Italian refugees, and French Socialists and Communists.

Throughout the winter and spring of 1937, the Nationalists continued their attacks around Madrid without success. Then they turned their attention to northern Spain, where the massive bombing of civilian targets was undertaken for the first time in Europe, most notably at Guernica.

Canadian volunteers on their way to assist Spain's democratic government in its fight with Franco.

Mackenzie-Papineau Battalion/Library and Archives Canada, C-067448.

Canadian Dr. Norman Bethune performs a blood transfusion on a badly wounded patient.

Geza Karpathi/Library and Archives Canada, C-067451.

Despite their government forbidding it, 1,600 Canadians travelled to Spain to fight for the Republic. They formed a unit named for the rebels of 1837, the Mackenzie-Papineau Battalion, and half of them died.

Perhaps the most famous Canadian to go to Spain was a doctor, Norman Bethune. Bethune led a mobile blood transfusion unit that worked close to the fighting and saved countless soldiers who might otherwise have died without his prompt treatment.

In 1937 Bethune returned to Canada and toured the country, talking to packed halls and hockey stadiums about Spain and raising money to help the Republic.

The Republic launched several offensives during 1937 and 1938, but they did not have the tanks, planes, artillery, or reserves of trained soldiers to hold any ground taken. As 1939 dawned, it was obvious that the Nationalists were winning. In April the Republic surrendered and Franco established a dictatorship that lasted until his death in 1975.

Terrified that a war as horrific as the Great War might break out if the war in Spain spread, Britain, France, the United States, and Canada introduced a policy of non-intervention to prevent any country from providing soldiers or weapons to either side.

The policy worked for the democracies, none of which supplied military help to either side. Unfortunately, Germany and Italy completely ignored non-intervention and supported Franco and his Nationalists. Italy supplied planes, tanks, and tens of thousands of regular soldiers. Germany supplied arms and an air force, the Condor Legion.

The ruins of Guernica. The Spanish army destroyed the undefended town with German support in 1937. The horror was later immortalized in a painting by Spanish painter Pablo Picasso.
Bundesarchiv.

The democracies went to extraordinary lengths to ignore what was happening in Spain. Time and again, the Spanish government and concerned neutral individuals presented solid information proving German and Italian involvement. It was all ignored.

Even when British merchant ships were attacked (more than 60 were attacked by Italian submarines and planes during the civil war, and more than 80 sailors killed), the only response from the non-intervention countries was more talking.

The Fascist countries saw the war in Spain as a chance to test their latest war machines and military tactics. What the Condor Legion learned over Guernica and Barcelona was put to use a few years later over Warsaw, London, and Coventry.

Despite overwhelming evidence of Fascist involvement in Spain, the democracies did nothing, missing an opportunity to send Hitler and Mussolini a strong message that their military ambitions would not be tolerated.

Only Mexico and the Soviet Union supported the Spanish Republic. Mexico was limited by distance and resources, and Stalin in Moscow had his own agenda. As the Spanish Civil War progressed, the Communists in the Republic became more powerful, eventually crushing any internal opposition.

Canada and the other democracies' failure to help the elected government of Spain against a military coup sealed the fate of the Republic. By the time Franco watched his victorious soldiers march through the streets of Barcelona and Madrid in 1939, the Spanish Republic was long dead and the war was between Fascism and Communism.

Non-intervention in Spain was not democracy's only spectacular failure in the years when the world seemed to be slipping almost inevitable toward another war.

STEPS TO WAR

As the 1930s progressed and no one stood up to Hitler, he became more confident. One of the Nazi aims had always been to incorporate the Germans in neighbouring countries into a "Greater Reich."

Many Germans outside Germany lived in Austria, a country created in 1919 from the ruins of the Austro-Hungarian Empire. They had never been a part of Germany but Hitler, who had been born in Austria, used Austrian Fascists to put pressure on the Austrian government. Eventually, on March 12, 1938, German troops crossed the border. They were met by flag-waving crowds and silence from the democracies.

Encouraged by the ease with which he annexed Austria, Hitler turned his attention to another Austro-Hungarian remnant, Czechoslovakia, where numbers of Germans lived

... a British Prime Minister has returned from Germany bringing peace with honour. I believe it is peace for our time.
— **Neville Chamberlain on his return from Munich**

We have suffered a total and unmitigated defeat ... This is only the first sip ... of a bitter cup which will be proffered to us year by year unless ... we arise again and take our stand for freedom.
— **Winston Churchill, denouncing the Munich Agreement**

The Munich Agreement is seen today as a shameful sellout of a small country. In retrospect, Churchill was right. However, in 1938 the agreement was met with relief and popular approval. Many people alive then had lived through the Great War and were prepared to do almost anything, including believing Hitler's claims that he wanted no more, to avoid a repetition.

There was another consequence of Munich that few knew about at the time. In 1938, within the German army

European leaders at Munich: (left to right) Neville Chamberlain of the UK, France's Édouard Daladier, Adolf Hitler, Benito Mussolini.
Bundesarchiv.

and military intelligence service, there had been a plan to overthrow Hitler if the Munich Crisis led to war with Britain and France. The sellout of Czechoslovakia removed the plotters' excuse for action and nothing was done. Had they gone ahead and succeeded, there might not have been a Second World War.

Neville Chamberlain, at Heston Aerodrome on September 30, 1938, holding the paper containing the resolution to commit to peaceful methods signed by both Hitler and himself.

Imperial War Museum collection No. D 2239.

in the border areas. Using the same tactics to stir up trouble, and claiming that the German minority was being mistreated, Hitler pressured the Czechs to give up their border areas.

Again worried about war, Britain and France attended a four-power conference with Germany and Italy in Munich (Czechoslovakia was not invited). On September 30, 1938, an agreement was signed giving the Czech border areas to Germany. Hitler swore he wanted no more, but in March 1939 German troops marched unopposed into what was left of Czechoslovakia. The Nazi Reich was growing alarmingly and no one was doing anything to stop it. Who would be next?

While the world worried about Hitler's territorial ambitions, he was busy consolidating his hold inside Germany. Dissidents were silenced by intimidation and violence, or were sent to the growing number of concentration camps being opened across the country. In Dachau and the other camps the inmates were worked, beaten, and sometimes killed.

Laws were introduced allowing for the forced sterilization of those considered undesirable: habitual criminals, the physically disabled, the mentally challenged or ill, and the deaf. This was the first step toward the later killing of those the Nazis thought didn't fit with their racial ideal.

The Nuremberg Laws for the so-called "protection of German blood and German honour" were passed in 1935. They defined being German as having four German grandparents, being Jewish as having three or four Jewish grandparents, and being "mixed blood" as having one or two Jewish grandparents.

These women are wearing the stars they were forced to don to identify themselves as Jews.
Bundesarchiv.

Not all Germans accepted what was going on in their country. Despite the failure of organized churches in Germany to oppose Hitler, a few brave men spoke out. The most famous was a Lutheran pastor, Dietrich Bonhoeffer.

Bonhoeffer spoke out and wrote against the Nazis' totalitarian and racial policies throughout the 1930s. Despite the chance to stay in the U.S. in 1939, he returned to Germany, where he joined the Abwehr, German military intelligence, as a double agent.

Bonhoeffer was arrested in 1943, but continued to make his views known through letters smuggled out of prison. At dawn on April 9, 1945, just two weeks before American troops arrived, Bonhoeffer and other dissidents were executed by hanging with piano wire at Flossenbürg concentration camp.

Dietrich Bonhoeffer.

The laws also deprived Jews of German citizenship and forbade marriage, or sexual relations, between Jews and Germans. Harsh though the Nuremberg Laws were, their real horror lay in the twisted definition they gave to being Jewish, which later allowed the Nazis to easily identify the millions of Jews who were to be murdered in the Holocaust.

The Nuremberg Laws: This chart explains the Nazis' twisted method for determining "purity" of a person's bloodline through the extent of their Jewish ancestry.

NORMAN BETHUNE

*I refuse to live in a world that spawns murder and corruption
without raising my hand against them. I refuse to condone,
by passivity, or by default, the wars which greedy men make
against others.*

— NORMAN BETHUNE, 1937

After his adventures during the Spanish Civil War, Norman
Bethune was not willing to settle back into being a doctor in
Montreal. He had seen the threat of Fascism first-hand and
knew he had skills that could make a difference. During his
cross-Canada speaking tour to raise money for the Spanish
Republic, he declared that he was a Communist and found

Dr. Norman Bethune on the Great Wall of China.
Library and Archives Canada, PA-161839.

another cause to dedicate himself to: Mao Zedong's struggle against the Japanese in China. In January 1938, he sailed for Hong Kong.

Mao's war was a guerrilla war, so Bethune developed a surgery that could be dismantled and loaded on the backs of a few mules when the Japanese threatened. Time and again, he operated while enemy shells landed around him and fighting raged in nearby hills.

One difficulty Bethune had was persuading the local peasants, who distrusted modern medicine, to give blood for his transfusion service. But he had a trick. When a soldier was brought into a village, pale, cold, and motionless, Bethune would theatrically call all the locals and give the man a blood transfusion. As the crowd watched in awe, the apparently dead man would quiver, open his eyes, and come back to life. Bethune never had trouble with blood donors after that.

Bethune became a hero to the Chinese people. This painting shows him performing a transfusion.
Library and Archives Canada, PA-157322.

Bethune lived a harsh, isolated existence through 1938 and 1939, working brutally long hours and unable to communicate effectively with those around him. By October 1939 he was exhausted and thinking of returning to Canada. He did not even know that the Second World War had broken out.

On October 28, Bethune cut his finger while operating on a soldier with a broken leg. The cut became infected and, with no antibiotics available, the infection raced through Bethune's weakened body. Early in the morning of November 12, in a remote village, while Chinese soldiers fighting the Japanese in the nearby hills shouted his name, Norman Bethune died.

Norman Bethune is not well-known in Canada, but he is revered by hundreds of millions in China. He is considered of "national historic significance," and every year hundreds of thousands of people visit his tomb and statue, across the road from the Norman Bethune International Peace Hospital in Shijiazhuang. Hundreds more travel to visit the house where he was born in Gravenhurst, Ontario.

In a very real sense, the Second World War was fought for oil. Japan, Italy, and Germany had no oil resources of their own, so they had to rely on other countries to supply the needs of their industries and armies. Each looked to the closest oilfields that they could control: Japan to the British-controlled oilfields in Burma, Italy to the European oilfields in Romania, and Germany to the oil reserves in the Caucasus of Russia. Sooner or later, those were the directions that these three aggressive countries would turn.

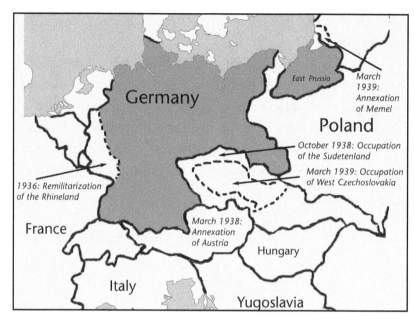

The European borders of 1939.

Few people celebrated New Year 1939 with any great hope that the fragile peace of the past 20 years would last much longer.

Japan was in the second year of a brutal, aggressive war in China, which was costing hundreds of thousands of lives and adding millions of new subjects and vast areas of territory to the expanding empire.

Italy had expanded its empire in Africa with a successful war in Ethiopia, and was planning the invasion of Albania. Mussolini was talking about recreating the ancient Roman Empire.

Germany was absorbing surrounding countries at an alarming rate. First Austria, then Czechoslovakia, and now Hitler was talking about Poland.

It was becoming strikingly obvious that the Western democracies were facing two choices: either allow Japan, Italy, and Germany to continue expanding, imposing their totalitarian regimes upon their neighbours and enslaving whomever they wished, or take a firm stand. It was never really a serious choice, only a question of what event would trigger the inevitable war, and when.

REARMAMENT

With war looming, everyone rushed to upgrade their armed forces. Germany, Italy, and Japan had been doing this for a long time, and Britain and France struggled to catch up. Everyone was busy developing and building bigger, faster, better bombers, fighter planes, tanks, battleships, and aircraft carriers. Ironically, the armaments boom helped the economies of these countries emerge from the slump of the Great Depression.

It wasn't just better machines that were important. If the horrors of trench warfare were not to be repeated, new tactics would be required.

Sherbrooke Fusiliers crew with a Sherman tank.
Library and Archives Canada, PA-130490.

In the 1920s theoreticians in Britain, France, Germany, and Russia came up with new ideas based on a Great War invention, the tank. Armoured vehicles could smash through defences, overwhelm infantry, and race into open country much faster than soldiers on foot. The difficulty was that tanks could be destroyed easily by well-placed artillery, and didn't carry enough firepower to compete with them. There was no point in having your tanks break through if they were going to be held up and destroyed by artillery over the next hill. The enemy artillery had to be destroyed quickly, but it took a long time to drag your own artillery up.

The answer, most effectively worked out by Germany, was artillery with wings — dive bombers. The German Stuka was a fearsome weapon. It could be called up by a halted tank commander and within minutes the distinctive dark, screaming shapes were dropping bombs with pinpoint accuracy. The Germans called the combination of tanks and dive bombers "lightning war" — or blitzkrieg.

Blitzkrieg was not a well-defined tactic that the German army employed deliberately in 1939. The term *blitzkrieg* was not even widely used until journalists picked it up after the war broke out. The theory of blitzkrieg was known, but the practicalities of integrating tanks, planes, and infantry as a unified whole were only developed in the field once the fighting actually began. Of course, the stunning success of blitzkrieg in the early days of the Second World War cemented it in people's imagination, and made it look as if it had all been carefully planned.

German Stukas over Poland, 1939.
Bundesarchiv.

By 1939 life in Germany, if you were Jewish, was close to unbearable. You had no rights, no job, and your property had been taken from you. Those who could, including Albert Einstein and Sigmund Freud, had fled. Others tried desperately, but it wasn't easy.

That June, 927 German-Jewish refugees sailed from Hamburg in the liner *St. Louis*. The United States, Columbia, Paraguay, Argentina, and Chile refused to allow them to land. Cuba took 22. The remainder returned to Europe.

Two hundred and eighty-eight were given refuge in Britain, the other 617 settled in Holland, Belgium, and France, all countries shortly to be invaded by Germany. As far as can be determined, of those 617, only 240 survived the war.

Jewish refugee children arriving in London, February 1939.

Another refugee program was more successful. Throughout 1939, Jewish and Christian charitable organizations in Britain organized the Kindertransport, the rescue of Jewish children from Austria, Czechoslovakia, and Germany. In all, 10,000 children found safety in Britain before the trains began rolling across Europe toward Sobibor, Treblinka, and Auschwitz.

One other refugee arrived in Britain that summer, Eduard Beneš, the president of Czechoslovakia before its conquest. He established the first European government in exile. Soon he would be joined by many more.

LAST SUMMER

In April 1939, Hitler's army marched unopposed into what was left of Czechoslovakia, and everyone finally knew for certain that he wasn't going to stop, regardless of how many concessions were made. But summer went on.

Every afternoon the Orient Express to Istanbul left London on its three-day journey through France, Germany, Austria, Hungary, Romania, and Bulgaria. If you were inclined to stop over in Berlin, guidebooks recommended a stroll along the tree-lined Unter den Linden.

Unfortunately, politics didn't take a rest that summer. Nazi-controlled newspaper headlines screamed about the threat that Poland posed to Germany's eastern frontier, and how harshly treated the Germans were inside the Polish border. The accusations were total fabrications, but Hitler told a League of Nations commissioner, "If the slightest incident happens I shall crush the Poles without warning in such a way that no trace of Poland can be found afterward." Hitler was determined to go to war with Poland. His only concern was what Russia, Poland's neighbour to the east, would do.

Poster for the Orient Express.

The world was shocked on August 23, when it was announced that Germany and Russia had signed a non-aggression pact (called the Molotov-Ribbentrop Pact). Fascism and Communism hated and feared each other, so why had they signed a treaty?

Russian foreign minister Vyacheslav Molotov signs the Molotov-Ribbentrop Pact, a German–Soviet non-aggression pact.

Stalin was worried about the strength of the German army and what might happen if it marched into Poland. Hitler was worried that if his aggression in Poland led to war, he might be facing Britain and France to the west and Russia to the east. Neither of them was ready to go to war just yet, but there was a secret map attached to the treaty. It showed a line down the middle of Poland. When Hitler invaded from the west, Stalin would move in from the east. Poland was to be cynically cut in half and divided between the two European powers.

Unaware of the map, President Roosevelt appealed for Germany and Poland to resolve their differences. On August 25, Britain signed a formal treaty with Poland, stating that if Poland were attacked Britain would come to her aid. Britain, France, and even Italy put pressure on Hitler, but his mind was made up.

On the night of August 31, German radio announced that a radio station had been attacked by Polish soldiers and a German killed. It was another lie: the Polish soldiers were Germans in fake uniforms and the dead German was a criminal shot by his own side.

The city of Wielurí in Poland after Luftwaffe bombing on September 1, 1939.

At dawn on September 1, German armoured units crossed the border into Poland. Above them a vast armada of aircraft swept east and bombs began to fall on Warsaw. On September 3, Britain and France declared war on Germany. On the 10th, Canada followed suit. The Great War had suddenly become only the first major war of the 20th century.

BEGINNINGS

September 1, 1939, is commonly taken to mark the beginning of the Second World War, but there are alternatives. Maybe we should consider the beginning to be the point when serious fighting between major participants in the war began. That would make the beginning 1937, when Japan invaded China, or perhaps 1931, when the Japanese invaded Manchuria. Alternatively, you can argue that the Second World War didn't really get underway until all the major participants were involved, which would make the start the Japanese attack on Pearl Harbor in December 1941.

Canadians land at Juno Beach on D-Day, June 6, 1944.

Lieutenant Richard Graham Arless/Department of National Defence/Library and Archives Canada, PA-182953.

There is yet another way of looking at it. Maybe there was no First or Second World War. Perhaps it was all the same conflict that began in August 1914 and ended in September 1945, and the years between 1918 and 1939 (or 1937 or 1941) were merely a truce while fighting went on on the sidelines in China and Spain, a breathing space while the major powers gathered their strength for the next round.

However you see it, the fragile peace that was created with such hope at Versailles in 1919 was doomed, and the world you and your parents grew up in would never be the same.

Whether the 21 years between the end of the Great War and the beginning of the Second World War were just a long truce or not, the peace of those years failed spectacularly. The war that followed was the largest, most costly, and horrendous one in human history. Somewhere between 60 and 70 million soldiers and civilians died, entire cities were almost completely obliterated, a nearly unimaginable, deliberate program of genocide was carried out, and the world emerged under the shadow of nuclear annihilation. Yet, in the almost 70 years since then, despite continual conflicts across the globe, nothing like a world war has broken out. Why was the peace of 1919 so fragile?

The answers are many and complex:

- The scale and horror of mechanized trench warfare left those who survived cynical about living in the best-of-all-possible worlds and the fundamental goodness of humans.

- Germany, the aggressor in both wars, was not convincingly defeated in 1918, at least from the perspective of many within the country.

- Terrifying revolutions, beginning with the one in Russia, swept across Europe. Although most failed, they left people with a sense of fear.

- The meltdown of the economic system, both in hyperinflation and later in the Great Depression, left people uncertain and insecure.

As a result, people looked for clear answers, a philosophy that promised security and simplicity, whether that lay to the left or right, Communism or Fascism. Polarization and extremism became the norm and the only way to resolve them was through war.

Fortunately, the major democracies, Britain, the United States, and Canada, finally managed to mobilize their will and resources to defeat the threat of totalitarianism, but that was by no means a certain outcome as the hope that the Great War would be the war to end all wars disintegrated.

Wars are simple: fight until someone wins and someone loses. Peace is tougher and more complex. When war breaks out, everyone loses. That is why the hope of peace is so often a failed hope.

Timeline

1918, January 8	President Wilson outlines his 14 points for peace.
1918, November 11	At 10:58 a.m., Private George Price dies in Villes-sur-Haime.
1918, November 11	At 11 a.m., the Armistice ends fighting in the First World War.
1918, November	Revolution breaks out and quickly spreads across Germany.
1919, January 15	Rosa Luxemburg and Karl Liebknecht murdered and the German Revolution is crushed.
1919, April 13	Amritsar Massacre in India.
1919, May 3	Munich Soviet Republic crushed.
1919, May 15	Workers go on strike in Winnipeg.
1919, May 21	Police charge crowd in "Bloody Saturday" in Winnipeg.
1919, June	First flight across the Atlantic by Alcock and Brown.
1919, June 28	Treaty of Versailles signed.
1919, August	Weimar Constitution signed into German law.
1919, October 28	Prohibition becomes law in the United States.
1919	Afghan War.
1919–1921	Irish War of Independence from Britain.
1919–1923	Russian Civil War.
1920	Red Army is defeated outside Warsaw.
1920	Iraqi revolt. The British put King Faisal on the throne.
1921, November 9	Mussolini forms the National Fascist Party in Italy.
1921–1923	Hyperinflation in Germany.
1922, October 27–29	The March on Rome. Benito Mussolini seizes power in Italy.

1922, November 4	Entrance to Tutankhamun's tomb discovered.
1922	Banting and Best discover insulin.
1922–1923	Irish Civil War.
1923, February 16	Foster Hewitt broadcasts his first hockey game on the radio.
1923, September 1	Great Kanto earthquake strikes Sagami Bay.
1923, November 9	Hitler's Munich Putsch fails.
1924, January 21	Vladimir Lenin dies, leaving the way open for Joseph Stalin to attain supreme power in Russia.
1925, June 7	Newfoundland Memorial unveiled at Beaumont-Hamel.
1925, July	Scopes trial in Tennessee.
1926, January 26	First public demonstration of television.
1927, May 20–21	Charles Lindberg become the first person to fly solo across the Atlantic.
1927	Mississippi River floods part of seven states.
1927	The Chinese Communist Party splits and begins the civil war.
1928, September	Okeechobee Hurricane.
1928	Percy Williams wins two gold medals at the Olympics.
1929, January 29	*All Quiet on the Western Front* published in Germany.
1929, February 14	St. Valentine's Day Massacre in Chicago.
1929, October	Stock markets crash, triggering the Great Depression.
1929, November 18	Grand Banks earthquake off Newfoundland.
1929	Graf Zeppelin circumnavigates the globe.
1930, March/April	Ghandi's Salt March to protest British taxes.
1930, September	The Nazi Party grows from 12 to 107 seats in the German parliament.
1930, October 5	Airship R101 crashes and burns in France.
1930	The drought that triggered the Dust Bowl begins.

1931, April 14	Spanish Republic declared in Madrid.
1931	Al Capone indicted and tried for income tax evasion.
1931	Japanese invade Manchuria and establish a puppet emperor.
1931	30,000 Americans die in automobile accidents.
1932, May 21	Amelia Earhart becomes the first woman to fly solo across the Atlantic.
1932, July 31	Nazis become the largest party in the German Reichstag.
1932	J.S. Woodsworth becomes leader of the new Co-operative Commonwealth Federation.
1933, January 30	Adolf Hitler is elected chancellor of Germany.
1933, March 4	Franklin Roosevelt becomes president and institutes the New Deal.
1933, March 22	Dachau opened.
1933, May 10	Students burn tens of thousands of "un-German" books in the streets.
1933, December 5	Prohibition repealed in the United States.
1934, May 23	Bonnie and Clyde killed in Louisiana.
1934, June/July	Hitler purges opposition within the Nazi Party in "The Night of the Long Knives."
1935, April	Relief camp workers in British Columbia strike and travel to Vancouver.
1935, June 3–4	On to Ottawa Trek begins.
1935, July 1	Police attack trekkers in Regina, effectively ending the protest.
1935, September 15	Anti-Jewish Nuremberg Laws announced in Germany.
1935, October 14	William Lyon Mackenzie King becomes prime minister of Canada.
1935, October	Italy invades Abyssinia.
1936, July 17–18	General Franco leads a military revolt against the Spanish Republic to begin the Spanish Civil War.
1936, July 26	Vimy Ridge Memorial unveiled.

1936, August 1–16	The Summer Olympics take place in Berlin.
1937, April 26	Guernica bombed.
1937, May	Mackenzie-Papineau Battalion of Canadian volunteers fighting for the Spanish Republic formed.
1937, May 6	The Hindenburg explodes while docking in New Jersey.
1937, July 2	Amelia Earhart disappears near Howland Island in the Pacific.
1937, July 7	Japan invades China.
1937, December	Japanese soldiers kill an estimated 300,000 civilians in Nanking.
1937	Norman Bethune tours Canada, raising money for the Spanish Republic.
1938, January	Norman Bethune sails for China.
1938, March 12	German troops enter Austria unopposed.
1938, September 30	The Munich Pact is signed, giving Germany the border areas of Czechoslovakia.
1938, November 9–10	Jewish synagogues, homes, and shops are attacked across Germany.
1939, March 15	German troops march into the remainder of Czechoslovakia.
1939, April	Italy invades Albania.
1939, June	927 Jewish refugees sail from Hamburg on the liner *St. Louis*.
1939, August 23	Germany and Russia sign a non-aggression pact.
1939, August 25	Britain signs a formal treaty with Poland.
1939, September 1	Germany invades Poland.
1939, September 3	Britain and France declare war on Germany.
1939, September 10	Canada declares war on Germany.
1939, September 17	Russia invades eastern Poland.
1939, November 12	Norman Bethune dies of blood poisoning in China.

Resources for Learning More about the Lost Peace

The following is a selection of the books used by the author in writing this story:

The Battle for Spain by Antony Beevor (New York: Penguin, 2006)

The Spanish Civil War by Hugh Thomas (New York: Penguin, 1965)

Canada: Our Century by Mark Kingwell and Christopher Moore (Toronto: Doubleday, 1999)

The Gallant Cause by Mark Zuehlke (Vancouver: Whitecap, 1996)

The Coming of the Third Reich by Richard J. Evans (New York: Penguin, 2003)

The Holocaust by Martin Gilbert (New York: Henry Holt, 1985)

The Rising Sun by John Toland (New York: Bantam, 1971)

The Timetables of History by Bernard Grun (New York: Simon and Schuster, 1975)

Hindenburg by Michael M. Mooney (London: Mayflower, 1974)

Weimar: A Cultural History by Walter Laquer (New York: Putnam, 1980)

Europe by Norman Davies (New York: Oxford University Press, 1996)

A History of the Twentieth Century: Volume 1, 1900–1933 by Martin Gilbert (New York: William Morrow, 1997)

A History of the Twentieth Century: Volume 2, 1933–1951 by Martin Gilbert (Toronto: Stoddart, 1999)

All Quiet on the Western Front by Erich Maria Remarque (London: Mayflower, 1963)

Internet Resources

If you want to learn more about some of the topics covered in *Failed Hope*, these websites are a good place to start.

www.nwbattalion.com
Check out the 28th (Northwest) Battalion Headquarters for more information on A Company.

cefww1soldiergprice.blogspot.ca/2007/05/last-canadian-killed-in-ww.html
More about George Price, the last Canadian killed in the First World War.

www.flamesofwar.com/hobby.aspx?art_id=573
History of the 2nd Canadian Infantry Division.

www.firstworldwar.com/bio/foch.htm
Biography of Ferdinand Foch.

www.indianchild.com/mahatma_gandhi.htm
A biography of Mohandas (Mahatma) Gandhi.

www.veterans.gc.ca/eng/memorials/ww1mem/vimy
More information about the Canada National Vimy Memorial.

www.veterans.gc.ca/eng/history/SecondWar
Information about Canada's role in the Second World War.

www.canadiangreatwarproject.com
A site that focuses on Canada's role and the impact of the war on the country.

Index

ABOUT THE AUTHOR

Born in Edinburgh, Scotland, John Wilson grew up on the Isle of Skye and outside Glasgow without the slightest inkling that he would ever write books. After obtaining a degree in geology from St. Andrews University, he worked in Zimbabwe and Alberta before taking up writing full-time and moving to Lantzville on Vancouver Island.

John is addicted to history and firmly believes that the past must have been just as exciting, confusing, and complex to those who lived through it as our world is to us. Every one of his books deals with the past. His tales involve intelligent dinosaurs, socialist coal miners, confused boys caught up in the First and Second World Wars, and the terrors faced by Arctic explorers. His novel *The Alchemist's Dream* was shortlisted for the Governor General's Award.

John has also written the *Weet* fiction series, as well as the Stories of Canada titles *Righting Wrongs: The Story of Norman Bethune, Discovering the Arctic: The Story of John Rae,* and *Desperate Glory: The Story of WWI.* The first two were shortlisted for the Norma Fleck Award for children's non-fiction and the last for the Red Maple Award. The follow-up to *Desperate Glory, Bitter Ashes: The Story of WWII,* was published in the fall of 2009.

By the Same Author

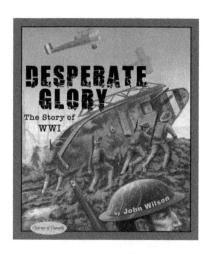

Desperate Glory
The Story of WWI
John Wilson
978-1-894917421
$20.95

This book presents the story and issues of the First World War in a clear, concise, and objective manner, accompanied on every page by photographs, original sketches, or maps. Focussing on social as well as political issues with a Canadian perspective, Wilson presents the issues of the war with depth and compassion. This book will be a very useful tool for educators in explaining the hows and whys of this most important period.

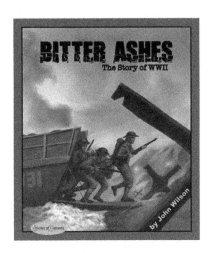

Bitter Ashes
The Story of WWII
John Wilson
978-1-894917902
$20.95

World War Two was the greatest conflict in human history. It gave birth to the Atomic Age, the Cold War, and the economic boom of the 1950s and 60s, and planted the seeds of today's Middle East crises. But it is not distant history. Most Canadians have relatives who were part of this world-wide tragedy. Bitter Ashes puts these events in context for them. This book in the illustrated historical series Stories of Canada is a companion to *Desperate Glory: The Story of WWI.* A clear and concise text leads the reader though the major military and political events and issues of the war. Sidebars add detail and a personal element. Every page is illustrated with either photographs or maps.

Available at your favourite bookseller.

VISIT US AT
Dundurn.com
Definingcanada.ca
@dundurnpress
Facebook.com/dundurnpress

FREE DOWNLOADABLE TEACHER RESOURCE GUIDES